NEW YORK REVIEW BOOKS

POETS

WANG YIN, born in Sh[a]... poetry in the 1980s, and w[as]... foremost writers of the Th[ird Generation, for posi-Misty]. As an art critic and reporter for *Southern Weekly*, China's leading liberal newspaper, he has traveled extensively in Europe and Asia. His photography, often documenting his engagement with contemporary artists and writers, has been exhibited in China and internationally. He has curated the international Poetry Comes to the Museum reading series at the Minsheng Museum in Shanghai since 2012, the longest-running poetry series in the country. Wang Yin's 2015 collection, *Limelight*, won two of China's top poetry prizes, and his poetry has been translated into French, Spanish, Japanese, and Polish, among other languages.

ANDREA LINGENFELTER is a translator, poet, and scholar of Sinophone literature. Her translations include *The Changing Room: Selected Poetry of Zhai Yongming* (Northern California Book Award winner), Wang Yin's *Ghosts City Sea*, Hon Lai Chu's *The Kite Family*, Li Pik-wah's (Lilian Lee) *Farewell My Concubine* and *The Last Princess of Manchuria*, and Mian Mian's *Candy* and *Vanishing Act*. Lingenfelter's poetry has appeared in *Plume*, *Asian CHA*, and other journals. She teaches both literary translation and the literature and film of the Asia-Pacific at the University of San Francisco.

ADONIS was born Ali Ahmad Said Esber in the Syrian village Al-Qassabin in 1930. In 1956, fleeing political persecution, he moved to Beirut. In 1985, the ongoing Lebanese Civil War forced him to relocate to Paris, where he has resided ever since. One of the most influential contemporary Arab poets, he is the author of numerous collections, a translator of Ovid and Saint-John Perse, and has received many honors, including the Ordre des Arts et des Lettres, the Goethe Prize, and the Pen/Nabokov Award.

Wang Yin

A Summer Day in the Company of Ghosts
Selected Poems

TRANSLATED FROM THE CHINESE
BY ANDREA LINGENFELTER

FOREWORD BY ADONIS

NYRB/POETS

nyrb   NEW YORK REVIEW BOOKS   *New York*

THIS IS A NEW YORK REVIEW BOOK
PUBLISHED BY THE NEW YORK REVIEW OF BOOKS
435 Hudson Street, New York, NY 10014
www.nyrb.com

Thanks to the following publications in which some of these translations
first appeared: *Granta*, *Manoa*, *The New York Times Magazine*, *Pathlight*,
Tupelo Quarterly, *Washington Square Review*, *Ghosts City Sea* (Seaweed
Salad Editions, 2021), and *Urban Poetry from China*, selected by Huang
Fan and James Sherry, translation editor Daniel Tay (Roof Books, 2021).

Library of Congress Cataloging-in-Publication Data
Names: Wang, Yin, 1962– author. | Lingenfelter, Andrea, translator. |
  Wang, Yin, 1962– Summer day in the company of ghosts. | Wang, Yin, 1962–
  Summer day in the company of ghosts. Chinese.
Title: A summer day in the company of ghosts / by Wang Yin; translated by
  Andrea Lingenfelter.
Other titles: Summer day in the company of ghosts (Compilation)
Identifiers: LCCN 2021056747 (print) | LCCN 2021056748 (ebook) |
  ISBN 9781681376486 (paperback) | ISBN 9781681376493 (ebook)
Subjects: LCSH: Wang, Yin, 1962—Translations into English. |
  LCGFT: Poetry.
Classification: LCC PL2919.Y448 S8613 2022 (print) |
  LCC PL2919.Y448 (ebook) | DDC 895.11/52—dc23/eng/20211206
LC record available at https://lccn.loc.gov/2021056747
LC ebook record available at https://lccn.loc.gov/2021056748

ISBN 978-1-68137-648-6
Available as an electronic book; ISBN 978-1-68137-649-3

Cover and book design by Emily Singer

Printed in the United States of America on acid-free paper.
10 9 8 7 6 5 4 3 2 1

Contents

**A SUMMER DAY IN THE COMPANY OF GHOSTS
(1990–1993)**

TO PENETRATE THEORY and teachings, and to practice an intimate coexistence with reality and its objects—this is a primary task in every original and creative poetic experience. And this is what Wang Yin expresses in his writing experience: he tears apart the veils that obscure reality. He cleanses words, washing the rust of modernity and postmodernity off of them, and builds his own poetic world in a space of childhood that embraces the world and its things, beyond technology in general, and beyond the machine in particular.

In his poetry, sight is more than merely seeing. It is also discernment, insight. For within the eye that sees, there is a second eye, one that thinks and meditates.

Thus, in his poetry, the poet appears as someone inventing an artistic alphabet wherein words are transformed into clouds pregnant with the rain of metamorphosis, wherein the body of matter is kneaded with an overflowing desire, and wherein a certain unity is achieved—the unity between

the clay of the object and the water of speech, between
imagination and the world.

And so it is that Wang Yin writes, mixing light and air,
he grants the rose its admirers, the machine its wings,
he wears the robe of space.

—Adonis
October 2021
Paris

Translated from the Arabic by Kareem James Abu-Zeid

> at first, what drew me in was a quality
> neither blankness   nor blackness
> and I cannot call to mind its name
> —Wang Yin, "Thing That's Not a Thing"

WANG YIN IS A POET of the ineffable. He is drawn to paradoxes, to the multiplicity and unknowability of the world around us. He is also a poet of witness, a historian of subjective experience. His poetry is marked by an intensity shaped by an acute awareness of ephemerality. At the same time, Wang Yin is a poet in the world, as cosmopolitan as his hometown of Shanghai. This collection does not attempt to unite these contradictions but rather to present this poet in all his complexity.

Born in Shanghai in 1962 into an intellectual and cosmopolitan family with roots in the literati heartland of the lower Yangzi, Wang Yin is both a writer and a traveler. He has remained in Shanghai while continually looking outward as well as inward in search of new inspiration.

Most critics classify Wang Yin as post-Misty. The Misty Poets (also known as the Obscure Poets) were part of the first generation of post-Mao writers. They rejected the simplistic boosterism and overt politics of socialist realism, which had dominated the cultural sphere under Mao into the mid-1970s. This trend reached its pinnacle of absurdity and brutality during the ten years of the Cultural Revolution. Breaking with this tradition, the Misty Poets were more concerned with inner turmoil than with class struggle—the authorities detested them, but people from all walks of life embraced their work, and they were wildly popular. Their work, influenced by translations of world literature that circulated after Mao's death, passed among friends and published in underground journals, was foundational for many so-called post–Misty Poets born ten to fifteen years later.

Wang Yin had something of a head start in reading international literature compared to many of his peers. When he was a child, in the early days of the Cultural Revolution, his family home was raided by Red Guards. They pulled the gold rings from his grandmother's fingers but left untouched an attic full of books—many of them works in translation. In spite of, or perhaps because of, his parents' repeated admonitions not to go to the attic, Wang Yin would sneak up to the family library as soon as his parents had left for work and were safely out of the house. He spent hours reading translations of European classics. Goethe's *Faust* made a particularly deep impression on him. It was not until much later in life that he developed an appreciation for classical Chinese literature.

A Summer Day in the Company of Ghosts: Selected Poems is the first comprehensive edition of Wang Yin's poetry in English and spans nearly forty years of his writing life. It follows the organization and ordering of his 2015 collected works, *Limelight/Greylight*, from which all but the fourteen pieces in the opening section of new poems have been selected.

The early poems of the 1980s, which comprise the fifth and sixth sections of this volume—"Recitation" and "House of Spirits"—reflect a restless and curious mind. Wang Yin writes about international literary and artistic icons like Robert Bly and Robert Capa, as well as Chinese antecedents like the progressive writer Lu Xun, who died of tuberculosis in Shanghai in 1936, and contemporaries such as the poet Liang Xiaoming. One of Wang Yin's best-known early poems is "Thinking About a Czech Film, but I Can't Remember the Title," an atmospheric blend of romanticism and veiled political commentary. "The English" and "Red Hotel" take the satire even further. Other poems in these two sections embrace surrealism, including the oddly poignant "Martians."

The original title for section three, "Limelight/Greylight" (灰光灯) was particularly tricky to translate. Wang Yin borrowed this literal translation of the English word for a bygone form of theatrical lighting from one of the early Chinese titles of Charlie Chaplin's 1952 film. Although in English the word "limelight" has long since passed into the realm of metaphor and is now almost wholly associated with attention-seeking, it originally referred to the actual mineral—lime, or calcium oxide—used to create a powerful illumination. The compound word for "limelight" in Chinese is made up of three characters: 灰 (*hui*) meaning "lime, ash, dust, or grey"; 光 (*guang*) meaning "light, brilliant, or ray"; and 灯 (*deng*) meaning "lamp, light, or lantern." Wang Yin was captivated by the paradoxical ambiguity embodied by this image as a source of both light and shadow—a light that contains darkness. Because these associations are lost in English, I have paired the descriptive coinage "Greylight" with the English title Wang Yin has long used in homage to Chaplin. For Wang Yin, the image of grey light, a diffused light compromised by shadows, is central to his work. And such a binomial translation of his singular title seems fitting for his multilayered poetry as a whole.

The poems in section four, "A Summer Day in the Company of Ghosts," confront trauma, both personal and historical. Pointedly, summer here is a season of mourning, a time for commemoration, for the poet to process grief and disillusionment. Section three, "Limelight/Greylight" comprises poems written in the 1990s through the early 2000s. Themes of loss and mourning continue from the earlier sections, as in the elegy "White Sea," which was adapted into a performance by a modern dance company in Switzerland. The first poem of the section, "Flying Towards a Borderland of Rain," was written in 2004, two years after Wang Yin bought a digital SLR camera and was sent to France by his employer, the progressive Guangzhou-based newspaper *South Weekend*. This trip was followed by many more, to Europe and North America—travel, along with photography, becoming important sources of inspiration for his poetry ever since. I first read this poem on a flight between Shanghai and rainy Seattle, not long after first meeting Wang Yin in the summer of 2007 through a Shanghai publisher. I connected immediately to the poem's deep imagery and mood of uncertainty.

Section two, "The Evening of My Life Has Come Too Late," dives deeper into Wang Yin's engagement with the wider world, while also offering tender glimpses of his private life. The poems in this section focus on love and friendship, as well as his travels. Mysterious paradoxes merge with a newfound sense of contentment.

The book opens with a group of new poems. Some are set far from Wang Yin's home in Shanghai, like "Winter in Katowice," while others turn to the people close to him, as in "For Peng Bo'er on Her Tenth Birthday." Other poems such as "Suddenly" and "Now" reinvent the surrealism of his earlier work. Wang Yin speaks of the importance of describing all of human experience, not just heroism and aspiration but weakness and ambivalence as well. Many of these poems show his acute awareness of the fragility and unpredictability of life, an awareness based on personal experience. In the late summer of 2008, he suffered two heart attacks, only a month apart. As he wrote in a 2016 acceptance speech, this brush with mortality "left me feeling intimate with happiness rather than terror. While I was recovering in the hospital, I went out every day to stroll and look around in a small nearby park. I would see others there wearing the same hospital pajamas as me, and their faces were inscribed with the desire to live. I also saw people writing on the pavement with brushes dipped in water, and there, in the sun and wind, those traces of water soon faded away until there was almost nothing left."

—*Andrea Lingenfelter*
November 2021
Kensington, California

New Poems

(2015–2021)

物非物

起初，吸引我的某种物质
不是空白　也不是黑暗
而是回忆不起它的名字

望见某种不明气味的形状
听得见无声的哭泣
却再也无法看见隐匿的泪水

深夜走过无人的街道
却说不清
这是在哪一座城市

我回避着阴郁的部分　却陷入了
低温下的美
恒温下的罪

2016

Thing That's Not a Thing

At first, what drew me in was a quality
neither blankness   nor blackness
and I cannot call to mind its name

Glimpsing a shape with an obscure scent
I can hear silent weeping
but will never again see those hidden tears

Walking down an empty street at night
I cannot say
what city this is

I've bypassed the depressing parts   but blundered
    nonetheless into
the beauty of frozen days
the blight of mild climes

2016

Translator's note: The title and content of this poem play on the Tang dynasty poem "Flower That's Not a Flower" by Bai Juyi. In Mandarin, the title of Wang Yin's poem reads *"wu fei wu"* (literally "thing that's not a thing"), which sounds exactly like the Mandarin reading of the second line of Bai Juyi's poem, 霧非霧 ("mist that's not mist").

你偏爱冷僻的词语

你已经感觉不到痛了
你也已经感觉不到冷了

你开始偏爱冷僻的词语
偏爱低产，偏爱均速，

你偏爱气泡水
你偏爱旧书的气味
偏爱昏睡，而不是清醒

你偏爱用听不见的声音读一首诗
用铅笔在纸巾上写下难以辨认的字迹
就像无法复原的破碎梦境

你已经感觉不到痛了
你也已经感觉不到冷了

你偏爱的春天也有阵亡的花朵
它们延续了上一季的寒意

2020

You Love Obscure Words

You no longer feel pain
and you no longer feel cold

You've started to love obscure words
to love low output and a steady pace,

You've come to love sparkling water
and the smell of old books
to love deep sleep, though your mind is cloudy

You love to recite a poem in a voice too quiet to hear
to leave indecipherable traces of characters penciled on
    paper towels
like a broken dream that can't be retrieved

You no longer feel pain
and you no longer feel cold

Your beloved springtime sees its blossoms fall in battle as
    well
they carry the chill of the season that came before

2020

卡托维茨的冬天

葬礼上下起了雨
悼念更缓慢了
小号手从小号里倒出更多的水
牧师和亡命徒的皮鞋
都陷在泥地里

冬天的第一个词是延迟
墓碑上找不到我的名字
我像6后面的7
不是被处决，就是被渴死

我宁愿此刻已是世界末日

2015

Winter in Katowice

During the funeral it starts to rain
the service slackens
the bugler dumps more water from his horn
and the priest's and the fugitive's leather shoes
sink into the mud

The first word of winter is delay
I can't find my name on any of these tombstones
I'm like the 7 after the 6
either executed or dead of thirst

If only this moment was the last day of the world

2015

你对我说，怀念那些缓慢的旧日子

你对我说，怀念那些
缓慢的旧日子
同样缓慢的自行车
和漏水的手表

我们都是不合时宜的人，端着不合时宜的咖啡
这一杯敬卡洛琳，这一杯敬贫穷
这一杯敬神经错乱的季节
这一杯敬无休无止的雪
敬过时的窃听器
最后一杯敬我们自己
这些不合时宜的人

你该知道，我多么乐意想象你
在一个极其陌生的城市
譬如耶路撒冷　譬如马拉喀什
或者那些我们都念不出地名的城市
好让我在走神的时候
在被雨淋湿的街道上与你不期而遇

所以，给你写信停笔的时候
就是我一如既往地走神
我发送电子邮件的瞬间，就是
无休无止的暴风雨
终于停歇的时刻

2015

You Tell Me You Miss Those Slow-Paced Days of the Past

You tell me you miss those
slow-paced days of the past
the equally leisurely pace of bicycles
and leaky wristwatches

We're both out of step with the times, lifting our
    old-fashioned cups of coffee
drinking a cup to Carolyn, another to poverty
drinking a toast to the season of mental confusion
another to the unrelenting snowfall
and another to the listening devices of yore
The last cup we drink is to ourselves
men out of step with the times

You should know how happy it makes me to imagine you
in an utterly unfamiliar city
like Jerusalem or Marrakesh, or Johnson, Vermont
or some other city whose name neither of us can pronounce
And someday when my head is in the clouds
I might happen to run into you on a rainy street

So when I pause for a moment while writing you
it's just me with my head in the clouds again
The moment I send the email, that's when
the relentless wind and rain
come to a halt at last

2015

突然

今天下午
巨大的海鸥
俯冲飞入步行街
发配到图书馆里的鱼
吃着水果

受伤的人抬着担架
走过街道

山坡上的雪入睡的时候
我们还醒着

今天下午
剿匪的夏天过去了

2016

Suddenly

This afternoon
a gigantic seagull
dive-bombed a pedestrian street
while fish exiled to the library for their crimes
were eating fruit

An accident victim carried a stretcher
down the road

When snow on the mountains drifts off to sleep
we will still be awake

This afternoon
a summer of reprisals drew to a close

2016

风可以隐藏(加尔各答)

风可以隐藏　　雾
可以隐藏　　但是
迟疑无法隐藏

只要我说加尔各答
你就会知道
我已经身在何处

就会知道火箭已经返航
会知道还有酒
酒的呼吸和温度

2015

Wind May Conceal (Kolkata)

Wind may conceal   mist
it may conceal   and yet
hesitation has nowhere to hide

I only have to say Kolkata
and you will know
where to find me

You will know the rocket has returned to base
and know there is still wine
the breath and warmth of wine

2015

现在

你开车把两个孩子带离了
春天病房，卧榻上的我试图
透过雾霾去看花园
却看到一场紫色的天花

在那里，天真的蜘蛛
生生死死，默默无闻，欢爱不息
衰弱的妹妹将空了的水杯
放在草地上

杯子压弯青草
就像那些往事需要有人提起
才能忆及子弹如何
洞穿羚羊的身体

即将到来的五月
兀自在鱼缸深处
梦见雨中那些
远离首都的甘蔗

2015

Now

You drive off with your two children, away
from the springtime ward, while I lie in bed
peering through smog for a glimpse of garden flowers
All I see is a field of purple roseola

There, innocent spiders
live and die in silence, happy as can be
A frail young woman sets an empty water glass
on the lawn

The glass bends the green blades beneath it
like past events you don't remember
until someone mentions them, like bullets
piercing the body of a gazelle

May, almost upon us
still deep in the fishbowl
dreaming of rain-soaked
sugarcane far from the capital

2015

阿肯的歌声

明亮的冬不拉
哀伤的霍布孜

阿肯的歌声
在特克斯河畔的草叶上
寻找闪亮的露水

燕隼去了，云还没来
骏马去了，风还没停

迷途的羊群在弓月道上
重逢无泪可流的故人

明亮的冬不拉
哀伤的霍布孜

阿肯的歌声
是那支越来越远的蜡烛
是那根越编越细的草绳

他们歌唱的是大雪纷飞
我听见的却是暴雨倾盆

2017.7

阿肯，哈萨克和吉尔吉斯对歌手的称谓aqyns.

Aqyn Songs

Bright dombyra
Mournful qobyz

The aqyns' songs
rove among grasses on the banks of the Tekes
searching for the sparkle of dew

The falcon has gone, the clouds haven't come
The stallion has gone, the wind hasn't calmed

Lost flocks of sheep on the crescent moon road
Old friends meet again, their tears long since spent

Bright dombyra
Mournful qobyz

The aqyns' songs
are candles that glow ever more distant
lengths of twine that grow thinner with every twist

Their songs are the roil of heavy snow
but all I can hear are torrential rains

July 2017

Author's note: Traditional Kazakh or Kyrgyz musicians participating
in aitys, oral poetry contests accompanied by dombyra or qobyz, are
called aqyns.

诗人的任务，在佛蒙特仿勃莱

正午之前
黑狗从草地上跑过
乔治在收拾窗下的花卉
他的太太坐在树下的靠背椅上
脸颊一阵灼热
阳光透过树叶缝隙射来
草地忽明忽暗
是浮云经过的时刻

除草机的马达声
无端惊醒本地的精灵
不该写久未写出的诗
和当地有关的诗
而是要侧耳倾听
万里之外
铁器碎裂的声音

2018

The Task of the Poet, Written in Vermont After Robert Bly

Not yet noon
A black dog comes running up the lawn
The gardener tidies up flowering shrubs under the windows
His wife sits in a chair beneath the tree
Cheeks suddenly burn hot as
Sunlight slips through the gaps between leaves
And the lawn flickers from light to dark
Marking the moment when clouds drift past

The sudden sound of the weed-cutter's motor
Breaks the reverie of the spirit of this place
I shouldn't write the poems I haven't gotten around to
    writing yet
Or poems about this place
Instead, I should open my ears and listen
To the cracking of iron
Thousands of miles away

2018

晚年涂鸦

用座标纸写信
给自己写信
给火焰写信
给宇航员写信
给不会回信的人写信

他们不说噪音　而关注寂静
不听惊雷　而只闻细雨
不问器官　只关心草木
不问生死　只专注僧侣
不问矿物　只关心哲学

为什么没有完成？
为什么要完成？
错误的不是城市　也不是国家
仅仅是夏末的尘埃
仅仅是暮色的峡谷
仅仅是被挥霍的天赋

2018

Chicken Scratches in My Twilight Years

Writing a letter on lined paper
Writing a letter to myself
Writing to a fire
Writing to an astronaut
Writing to someone who will never write back

They don't speak of loud voices   but closely observe the
    silence
They don't hear claps of thunder   but listen to the gentle
    rain
Rather than ask after your health   they care only for
    trees and grasses
Rather than ask about life and death   they look to men
    of the cloth
They don't ask about minerals   they care only about
    philosophy

Why isn't it completed?
Why does it have to be?
The fault is not the city   nor is it the nation
It's merely the dust of late summer
just a ravine in the dusk
nothing more than the squandered gifts of heaven

2018

给彭波而十岁生日

十年前，你来到人间
十年后，你将长大成人

不管未来如何被巨大的荒谬环绕
你都会记得今天早晨
歌唱的鸟儿比你更早地醒来

这些不是意外，也不是巧合
只有那些无形之物和未知之事
才能为我们解释美和欢乐

2019.4

For Peng Bo'er on Her Tenth Birthday

Ten years ago, you arrived in the human world
Ten years from now, you will be an adult

Even if the future finds you encircled by immense
    absurdities
may you still remember this morning
how the songbirds awakened even earlier than you

It isn't the exception, nor is it an accident
Only these things without form, these events yet unknown
can give us an account of beauty and joy

April 2019

恶作剧

这是两个
老死不相往来的仇敌
他们的诗集
却在书架上成为邻居

就像把他们紧挨着
葬在一起

2021.3.13

Prank

Here they are, two
lifelong enemies who never cross paths
Volumes of their poems
have become bookshelf neighbors nonetheless

It's as if they'd been pressed close
and buried together

March 13, 2021

爱情简史

你有时候需要生一场病
需要哭一哭　彻底哭出来
而不仅仅是
深夜里找人倾诉

你需要去潜水
去结识那些昼伏夜行的海盗
而不仅仅是待在旅馆的顶层
治疗久治不愈的失眠

你需要喜欢忧愁胜过喜悦
而不是在上海回到上海
你需要忘记吃药
只有在忘记的时候才会记得它

就像面对
猝不及防闪亮的灯塔

2021

A Brief History of Love

Sometimes you need a bout of illness
need to cry and cry   cry it all out
though it's nothing but
finding a shoulder to cry on late at night

You need to plunge underwater
get to know the night-marauding pirates who hide out by
     day
though it's nothing but loitering on the hotel rooftop
to cure the insomnia you've been trying to shake

You need to like it when sadness prevails over joy
and when you're not in Shanghai you have to return
You need to forget to take your medications
It's only forgetting that lets you remember

It's like being face to face
with a lighthouse that flashes without warning

2021

俳句的阿司匹林

夜航

航空椅背后的电视屏幕上
只有一架飞机
在地球的表面缓慢地移动

而你就在这架飞机上

电梯

穿工装的男人提着斧子
走进电梯，站在你的背后
电梯下得太慢了

地图

即使再熟悉不过的祖国地图
如果标上异国的文字
也立刻变得陌生了

Haiku Aspirin

NIGHT FLIGHT

On the seatback screen
nothing but an airplane
moving slowly over the surface of the earth

And you are on that very plane

ELEVATOR

Holding an axe, a man in coveralls
steps into the elevator and stands behind you
The elevator descends too slowly

MAP

A map of the homeland you know by heart
labeled with a foreign script
becomes instantly strange

蚂蚁

屋顶上那只红色的蚂蚁
在写明信片
无人知道是否能够收到

故乡

衣衫褴褛的早晨
如此亲切
好似故乡

钥匙

找到了钥匙
却遗失了锁
春天先到了南方

大鸟告诉我的一则故事

失眠已久的戏剧导演
只有在剧场里
才能睡个好觉

ANT

The red ant on the rooftop
is writing a postcard
No one knows if it will be delivered

HOMETOWN

Morning in its shabby clothes
as dear to me
as my hometown

KEY

I found the key
but lost the lock
Springtime comes first to the South

A STORY BIG BIRD TOLD ME

The director with chronic insomnia
only sleeps soundly
in a theater

夏天

一首诗重复着所有的诗
就像每一个秋天
都喜欢夏天的伤口

苹果

削完一只苹果
就听见远方的苹果树
轰然倒下的声音

2021

SUMMER

A poem repeats every poem
just as every autumn
adores summer's wounds

APPLE

After peeling an apple
I heard a distant apple tree
topple with a crash

2021

The Evening of My Life Has Come Too Late

(2015–2021)

此刻无须知晓生死

星光暗着，却看得清
你闪亮的嘴唇和眼睛
你一手抱着膝盖，一手
端着咖啡，等待水温变凉

我倚靠着熟睡的石头，听着
不安的蝉鸣掠过你的脊背
就像看你在雨后潮湿的
窄巷里艰难地倒车

也许揉皱的衣服应该再熨一下
也许应该再次拨动夏季的时针
咖啡杯里荡漾的图案
是你我无法预设的结局

这世界已经坏得无以复加，我们
只是侥幸在这空隙短暂停留
此刻无须知晓生死
只有走廊里的灯光依然灿烂

2011.6.25

For a Moment We Can Lose Consciousness of Life and Death

Starlight dims, yet even so, I still can see
the gleam of your lips and eyes
One of your hands clasps your knee, the other
holds a cup of coffee, as you wait for it to cool

I lean back against a sleeping stone, listen
to the restless chafing of cicadas brushing past your back
and it's like watching you drive in reverse
down a narrow alley after the rain

Maybe these wrinkled clothes need ironing again
Maybe the hand on summer's clock needs to be reset
The design floating in the coffee
is a resolution neither you nor I could ever predict

This world is too broken to restore, and we
are here only by chance, lingering briefly in this interval
For a moment we can lose consciousness of life and death
Only the lamps in the passageway are still burning

June 25, 2011

幽暗中的人弹着吉他

幽暗中的人弹着吉他
吟唱的是红色的花朵
也许是郊外摇曳的罂粟
也许是另一种不知名的花

有松树的庭院，黎明时分
落满松果，孔雀在花园里踱步
一把黑伞一顶帽子
沉在水池底部

午夜的雪花从桥下涌起
漫过头顶，升上星空
它们从高处俯瞰城市
就像格列柯一样

郊外开满了猩红的花朵
幽暗中的人弹着吉他
你摘下的珍珠耳环
在桌面上来回滚动

它们互相撞击的声音
微乎其微，就是罂粟
摇曳地开放，就是有人
再次拨响了幽暗的吉他

2015.5.19

In the Darkness, Someone Is Playing Guitar

In the darkness someone is playing guitar
singing of red roses
or swaying poppies in the countryside
or maybe some other nameless flower

A courtyard with pines, at first light
filled with fallen pinecones, sparrows hopping
a black umbrella and a hat
lying submerged at the bottom of the pond

Midnight snowflakes billow up from the bridge
rising above my head, into the starry sky
They look down on the town from on high
like El Greco

The countryside blooms with blood-red flowers
Someone is playing guitar in the dark
The pearl earrings you took off
roll around the tabletop

Bumping into each other, the pearls make
the faintest of sounds—it's the poppies
swaying open—it's someone
strumming a guitar again in the dark

May 19, 2015

昨夜下着今天的大雨

昨夜下着今天的大雨
冰冷的天赋一样美丽
城市此刻隐含着悲伤
琴匣里留下了玻璃的灰烬

飞艇的命名一再延迟
我依然不知道声音的颜色
一定要走到世界的尽头
天使的泪水才会模糊了大海

嘴唇下的秘密贴紧狂风
不是钥匙，也不是火焰
不是星光里的羞怯，更不是
今夜下到明天的大雨

2011.2.22

Today's Heavy Rain Poured Down Last Night

Today's heavy rain poured down last night
a gift from heaven, cold and beautiful
The city is harboring grief
traces of glass turned to ash in a violin case

The naming of the airship repeatedly postponed
I still don't know the color of its sound
We'll have to journey to the end of the world
for the angels' tears to blur the sea

The secret on my lips is close to madness
It's neither key nor spark
It's not the shyness of starlight, much less
tonight's heavy rain that falls into tomorrow

February 22, 2011

你的头发

它比我的头发柔软
也比我的头发纤细
我的毛衣上有你的头发
这是你昨夜留下的，我确认无疑

我试图抚平弄直它
然后把它放在白色的纸上
只要一离开我的手
你的头发立刻弯成美丽的曲线

就像用铅笔在纸上画出
你脸部的剪影
你的鼻子你的嘴唇
我长久亲吻过的部分

在冬夜呼啸来临的时候
我把你的头发
缠绕在左手食指上
你的体温渗透进我的骨髓

我把你的头发
夹在你的书里
这根头发上也有了
你身体深处的味道

2011.11.27

Your Hair

It's softer than mine
and finer than mine
that strand on my sweater
You left it last night, I am sure

I try to smooth it into a straight line
and lay it on a sheet of white paper
but the moment it leaves my hand
your hair arcs itself into a beautiful curve

as if I had sketched with pencil and paper
a line drawing of your face
your nose your lips
where I lingered in a long kiss

When the winter night came howling in
I took that strand of your hair
and wrapped it around my left index finger
and the warmth of your body seeped into my bones

I pressed your hair
into your book
This strand of hair also carries the scent
of the deepest places within your body

November 27, 2011

你为什么围绕着我旋转

你为什么围绕着我旋转
——霍夫曼斯塔尔

亲爱的阳光，我的蝴蝶
你为什么围绕着我旋转
我的诗篇是马背上犹豫的盐粒
是旅途中沉默寡言的邮差

我认识的蓝色阴影
潜行在白色岩石的下方
海洋如同月光一样明亮
天堂总是不在上帝这一边

雨点带着雨的气息
不断折入过去，季节的
疾病在我的窗外忽热忽冷
紊乱的玻璃也是真理

我喜欢陈旧的照片
习惯在电影院里重温时间
如水的巴赫，如雪的肖邦
这忧愁，这米酒是同一种黑暗

琴键上的黑人看不见飞扬的尘土
失明的飞鸟历数芬芳
倾斜的光芒依然无法
越过黑夜缓缓苏醒

2011.2.14

Why Are You Circling Around Me

Why are you circling around me
—Hugo von Hofmannsthal

Beloved sunshine, my butterfly
Why are you circling around me
My poems are flecks of salt clinging ambivalently to a
    horse's back
They're a taciturn postman out on his rounds

Familiar blue shadows
skulk along the base of a white boulder
The ocean shines like the moon
and Heaven is never where God is

Raindrops breathe with the rain
slipping into the past uninterrupted, and the season's
affliction blows hot and cold outside the window
Those smeared panes are another kind of truth

I like photos that are old and worn
I'm used to reviewing time in movie houses
Bach is like water, Chopin is like snow
This sadness and this rice wine are the same kind of
    darkness

The black man at the piano can't see swirling dust
Blind birds count out aromas
Slanting light still cannot
traverse the night's slow awakening

February 14, 2011

黑暗中的花瓣上升得如此之快

黑暗中的花瓣上升得如此之快
越过我们的肩膀
越过我们的瞳仁
超过我们的预期
也超过我们的惊慌和忧虑

黑暗中的花瓣上升得如此之快
是因为无休无止的迷雾
还是因为此刻你握着我的手
是因为音乐中蕴藏着无法知晓的秘密
还是因为幸福的泪水无处不在

2011.8.9

Petals in the Darkness Rise So Fast

Petals in the darkness rise up so fast
past our shoulders
past our pupils
surpassing our expectations
our anxiety and panic

Petals in the darkness rise up so fast
Is it because of the interminable fog
or because you're holding my hand
Is it because the music holds an impenetrable secret
or because we are engulfed in tears of joy

August 9, 2011

北方的海边生长着三棵松树

北方的海边生长着三棵松树
强劲的海风控制着它们的高度
就像被理发师不断修剪的头发
横向生长的松树有着扁扁的树冠

堤岸。海洋。灯塔。海岸线上
只有三棵低矮的松树
这寒冷地带的树木
在幽暗的树枝上结着硕大的松果

高跟鞋的后跟在沙滩上刻下深深的足印
夏天的男孩在树下甩出鱼钩
缺了鱼头的死鱼和冲上岸的
贝壳再也无法回到海里

我不知道北方海边的这三棵松树
在冬天的时候会是什么样子
贝壳会不会继续在沙滩上死去
灰色的海浪会不会一直拍打到松树的脚下

我只知道我在遥远的东方
梦着我的爱情,也许某一天
低头的时候,我会突然想起这三棵松树
在布列塔尼荒凉的海滨

2010.7.8

Three Pines Grow on a Northern Shore

Three pines grow on a northern shore
Strong winds constrain their height
Like hair under a barber's constant scissoring
these pines grow horizontally, flat-crowned

Beach. Ocean. Lighthouse. Coastline.
Only three stubby pines
These trees of the cold zone
sprout huge cones on their dark branches

High heels carve divots in the sand
Summertime and boys are casting fishhooks from under
    the trees
The headless fish and seashells flung
to the shore can never return to the sea

I don't know how these pines on this northern shore
might look in the winter
if the mussels will still be dying on the beach
if the grey waves will still be striking beneath the feet of
    these trees

I only know that far away, in the East
dreaming of my love, I may someday
lower my head and suddenly think of these three pines
on the wild shores of Brittany

July 8, 2010

晚年来得太晚了

晚年来得太晚了
在不缺少酒的时候
已经找不到杯子，夜晚
再也没有了葡萄的颜色

十月的向日葵是昏迷的雨滴
也是燃烧的绸缎
放大了颗粒的时间
装满黑夜的相册

漂浮的草帽遮盖着
隐名埋姓的风景
生命里的怕、毛衣下的痛
风暴聚集了残余的灵魂

晚年来得太晚了
我继续遵循爱与死的预言
一如我的心早就
习惯了可耻的忧伤

2011.6.6

The Evening of My Life Has Come Too Late

The evening of my life has come too late
There's wine in abundance
but no cups to be found, and nightfall
has drained the grapes of their color

October sunflowers are stunned raindrops
smoldering silks and satins
Magnified grains of time
fill the photo album of night

Bobbing straw hats screen off
a landscape gone incognito
the fear that haunts life, the pain beneath a sweater
The storm gathers to it every scattered soul

The evening of my life has come too late
I still abide by prophecies of love and death
just as my heart long ago
became inured to grief and its shame

June 6, 2011

昨夜有雨，今晨有雾

昨夜有雨，今晨有雾
海水太冷，白天太长
我仿佛看见你的夜航
在北方白色的海上

看不见鱼的海洋
听不见水的声音
没有眼睛的天空之下
冰封的海洋就是一方墓石

我们开始旅行，却不在同一海域
我们靠近大海，却不在同一艘船上
把我们分开的夏天无穷无尽
只有炽热的雨水还在不停地燃烧

天赐的黑暗总是突然抵达
遮蔽的不仅是六月的寒冷
我在昏暗的房间里关了灯
只是为了把黑夜看得更远

2010.10.18

Rain Last Night, Mist This Morning

Rain last night, mist this morning
the ocean too cold, the day too long
I thought I saw your night ship
on the white sea of the North

An ocean of fish I can't see
sounds of water I can't hear
Beneath an eyeless sky
the icebound sea is a gravestone

We begin our journeys, but on different seas
Each near an ocean, but aboard different ships
The summer that separates us has no end
There's nothing but hot rain that keeps on burning

Heaven's gift of darkness always arrives suddenly
It conceals more than the chill of June
In the gloom of my room I turn out the light
so that I might see farther into the dark night

October 18, 2010

那一片蓝色

那一片蓝色，那一片
如此接近蓝色的颜色
仅仅是一片蓝色，灰绿色的风
如期而至。就像婚礼前运到的一幅画
人们来到海边，停下脚步
蝴蝶撞到玻璃墙上
面对悬崖，沉默不语
为了避免迷失，他们陷入更深的迷失
这只是世界的一部分，心的一部分

这是布列塔尼
这是圣纳泽尔

你从未喜欢过海，从未想过
去捕捉风的踪迹
与它一起漂流
你想到星期六的婚礼
琢磨餐桌上的纸巾要怎样折叠
明天将要送来的餐桌
该怎样放在陆战队士兵
举行过升旗仪式的空地上

That Expanse of Blue

That expanse of blue, that expanse
of color so close to blue
is just an expanse of blue, with grey-green wind
blowing at the usual time, like a painting delivered before
    a wedding
People come to the seashore, stop in their tracks
butterflies knocking against a glass wall
facing tall cliffs, they have nothing to say
trying not to lose their way, they wander farther off the
    path
This is only one piece of the world, one piece of a heart

This is Brittany
This is Saint-Nazaire

You never liked the sea, never wanted to
chase traces of the wind
and drift on the breeze
You think about the wedding on Saturday
ponder how the paper napkins on the banquet tables
    should be folded
and how the tables that will be delivered tomorrow
should be laid out where squadrons of marines
once held flag-raising ceremonies

海与陆地，是两个接壤的国家
在它们的边境线上，你不会
找到自己的名字
那些在海底消失的潜艇
那些反复涂改的痕迹
在海滩上亲吻的人们
舞蹈的纸牌、烤玉米的小贩
旋转木马和手风琴手
都渺无踪迹，只有笨拙的
小丑躺在海滩上
不知所措

早晨的海穿着白色的袜子
海浪用唇语口述秘密
它的咽喉，哑了又哑
它是陌生的星球
瞬间苍老，转瞬年轻
你忘记了诸神的名字
却记住了灯塔的喘息
这已足够，人生太短
为什么还要羞惭

这不是圣纳泽尔
也不是布列塔尼

2014.7

56

Sea and land, two countries with a common border
There, along the line of their boundary, you cannot
find your name
the submarines lost at the bottom of the sea
the ever-vanishing tracks
the people kissing on the beach
dancing streamers, vendors selling roasted corn
merry-go-rounds and accordion players
All are gone without a trace, leaving just a clumsy
clown reclining on the beach
fresh out of ideas

The morning sea wears white socks
The waves whisper secrets
their throats are hoarse and getting hoarser
It's an unfamiliar planet
grown suddenly old, then suddenly young
You've forgotten the names of all the gods
but you remember the lighthouse catching its breath
That should be enough, life's too short
Why would you still feel ashamed

This isn't Saint-Nazaire
nor is it Brittany

July 2014

巴黎已经令我心生厌倦

能请你把音乐关了吗？
能让这屋子里只剩下黑暗吗？
请让我闭上双眼
放过这些无助的夜晚
让我能够听得到你起伏的呼吸

下午的天空突然变暗
海面突然有了阴影
所以，并不一定是在雨天
你才会在手心缓缓
转动这只黑色的杯子

你需要同一种颜色
只是黑色，就像这药片的底色
你让我接受了我的脆弱
我明白你担忧的黑夜是什么颜色
是什么颜色？
是这样的颜色吗？
是这些吗？
是吗？
是吗？

I've Had Enough of Paris

Can I ask you to turn off the music?
So that nothing is left in this room but darkness?
Please let me close my eyes
and let go of these helpless nights
Just let me listen to the rise and fall of your breathing

The afternoon sky turns suddenly dark
the surface of the sea suddenly in shadow
So it's not only on rainy days
that you turn this black cup
slowly in your hands

You need a color like that
Black, like the inside of this pill
You let me accept my own weakness
and I understand the colors of your melancholy nights
What colors are they?
These colors?
Those colors?
Are they?
Are they?

"六月，播种向日葵的季节
尼斯的向日葵还埋藏在地下……"
纽约的来信只有只言片语
原来七月才是开始
我远离祖国，远离盛夏
也远离了你，巴黎
已经令我心生厌倦

2013

"June, the season for sowing sunflower seeds
The sunflowers in Nice are still buried underground..."
A letter from New York is sparing in words
July turns out to be the beginning
I'm far from home, far from high summer
and far from you, and Paris—
I've had enough of Paris

2013

雨滴中的一滴雨

那一年冬天之后，再无大雪
只有连绵的阴雨
雨正在吃掉潮湿的报纸
正在吃掉我的嘴唇

一把雨伞、几滴昏迷的雨
雨点打在装花生的塑料袋上
就像我的另一个心脏正在跳动
我体内那个陌生的姐妹正在复活

那不是哀愁，那只是夜色中
一绺一闪而过的马鬃
只是不合时宜的停顿
只是雨滴中的一滴雨

2012.3.6

A Drop of Rain Inside a Raindrop

After that winter, there were no more big snows
only constant rain and heavy clouds
Rain eats away a sodden newspaper
eats away my lips

An umbrella, a few stunned raindrops
striking a plastic bag of peanuts
beating like my second heart
strange sister inside my body, coming back to life

This isn't sorrow, it's just the nighttime
flash of a horse's mane
It's just an untimely pause
a drop of rain inside a raindrop

March 6, 2012

喝过咖啡的下午

喝过咖啡的下午
喝过下午的咖啡
当风不再想到自己，阵雨
削弱了走廊深处的反光

尘埃的肖像上
有着南方黝黑的嘴唇
母亲的手帕载着
弥留的火车远去

我们有幸生活在
腐败的人们中间
你再一次攫住杯沿
畅饮荒谬的河流

喝过咖啡的夜晚
寂静终于到达终点
我顺从世俗的陋习，只有
你和半疯的雨在黑暗中躺下

2011

The Afternoon We Had Coffee

The afternoon we had coffee
we drank afternoon coffee
When the wind forgets itself, rain showers
whittle away reflected light in the recesses of corridors

On snapshots of dust
the inky lips of the south
Mother's handkerchief carries
dying trains on their distant journey

We are lucky to live among
this decadent crowd
Once again you grab the edge of the cup
and drink your fill of this ridiculous river

The night we had coffee
loneliness came to an end at last
I go along with the world's corrupt habits, only
you and the half-crazy rain lie down in the darkness

2011

你来到了孤单的巴黎

飞舞的灰烬总是时睡时醒
就像春天永远时喜时悲
除了拒绝还是拒绝
疼痛不再是最致命的恐惧

不安的闪电如同叹息
不对称的黑暗就像绝望的爱情
无知的肉体徒劳地远行
灰色的深处依然还是灰色

你来到了孤单的巴黎，沉睡的脸上
看不到苍茫寂寥的痕迹，除了脆弱
除了你沉默的手指
你疼痛得已了无知觉的内心

2005

You've Come to Lonely Paris

Windblown ashes always sleep fitfully
as spring forever wavers between sorrow and joy
To reject refusal is still a refusal
Pain can never be the most fatal terror

Restless lightning resembles sighs
asymmetrical darkness like unrequited love
Oblivious, the corporeal body journeys far, and for nothing
Grey depths remain grey all the same

You've come to lonely Paris, your sleeping face
bears no trace of boundless desolation, and other than
    fragility
other than your speechless fingers
your pain has reached your unfeeling psyche

2005

你是一座雾中的机场

你是一座雾中的机场
你的大腿为我的灵魂导航
你的嘴唇，我的眼睛
我们的旗语永远是沉默的海洋

你是一座低语的教堂
你的舞蹈割开黑色的露水
我是双脚赤裸的修士
乘坐木船穿过午夜的心脏

你是一座不眠的铁矿
你的嘴唇是我炽热的麦片
我的眼睛是你忧愁的火焰
我的手睡在你的手上

2006

You Are an Airport in the Fog

You are an airport in the fog
your thighs pilot my soul
your lips, my eyes
our semaphore will always be a silent sea

You are a whispering church
your dancing slices through the black dew
I am a barefoot monk
sailing a wooden boat through the carnal heart of midnight

You are an iron mine that never sleeps
your lips are my red-hot oatmeal
my eyes are your sorrowful flames
my hand sleeps on yours

2006

这是最黑的黑

这是最黑的黑
穿过黑暗看不见
脚背上的沙子
也看不见颤栗的影子
只有盐粒一般密集的星光
在头顶高处漂浮

昨天以后，明天以前，
每天都有同样的错误
在不断重复
那些光芒
那些转瞬即逝的光芒
那些转瞬即逝的不可靠的光芒
已经出发

这些突然启动加速的闪亮颗粒
是快速移动的飞行器
还是星际本身
失聪的耳语
永远像闪电一样热
像火一样冷

This Is the Blackest Black

This is the blackest black
I cannot see through this darkness to
the sand that covers my feet
Nor can I see the wavering shadows
only dense stars like grains of salt
floating overhead

After yesterday, before tomorrow,
every day marked by the same mistakes
and endlessly repeating
their radiance
their fugitive radiance
Their fugitive and unreliable radiance
has already left

Rapidly accelerating, flickering specks, are they
speeding airships
or the silent whispering of
interstellar space itself
perpetually hot as lightning
and cold as fire

如果环绕着微尘和我们的星空
突然四分五裂
如果它们没来由地突然崩塌
洞窟里那些没有名字的佛像
依然没有疼痛
身首异处的佛像
不会被再次征服
只有我们将不再是我们
诗人多多、剑钊、蓝蓝、叶舟和我

2010.6

If the starry sky that surrounds the dust and us
was suddenly rent apart
if it all collapsed without warning
the nameless buddhas in the caves
would not feel any pain
Those headless buddhas
cannot be conquered again
It is only we who can never be ourselves again
we poets Duo Duo, Jian Zhao, Lan Lan, Ye Zhou, and I

June 2010

Limelight / Greylight

(1993–2004)

飞往多雨的边境

飞往多雨的边境
波音757以僵硬的姿态
在飞行中获得休息
纸制的幻想和我并排坐着
观看一场两小时的电影
蓝色的空姐递上冰镇的可乐
果冻在锡箔纸里微微颤抖
机翼赤裸着骨头
宁静的引擎哗哗不休
我所不熟悉的风在舷窗外撕扯着什么
钉在水面上的钉子继承者忧虑和不安
我脚下的某处，载货卡车满载着铁矿石
排成长长的行列

是子夜，也是凌晨
月亮向我们转身而去
不安的碗，精致闪亮的表面
满含怀乡的幸福
哭泣停止了疼痛
这犹豫如此长久
几乎纠缠了我的一生
拉机场上空的浮云
弯曲下垂的星辰
和我一起
飞往多雨的边境

2004

Flying Towards a Borderland of Rain

Flying towards a borderland of rain
the Boeing 757 in its rigid pose
steals some rest in flight
Paper phantoms sit beside me
watching a two-hour movie
The blue stewardess hands me an ice-cold cola
Jello quakes faintly in a foil cup
The wings expose their bones
placid engines drone on and on and
unfamiliar winds outside the window tear things apart
Nails stuck to the water inherit our disquiet
Somewhere beneath my feet, trucks hauling loads of iron ore
have formed a long, long line

It's midnight, and it's nearly dawn
The moon turns its back on us and leaves
Troubled bowl, its fine surface
brimming with homesick joy
Tears bring an end to pain
This endless ambivalence clings to me
It's plagued me nearly all my days
Drifting clouds above the junkyard
Suspended stars twist and turn
along with me
flying towards a borderland of rain

2004

白色的海洋

白色的海洋穿过黎明的医院
裸露的玻璃尚有余温
我躺在潮湿的人行道上
水泥地面像镜子一样冰冷，城市
在我的脊柱之下
无声无息地运行

在悲伤的底层
不是夜晚又能是什么
我的沉睡唤作沉睡
我的哭泣是所有的哭泣
抒情的润滑剂
打开谎言的盖子

宇宙这样易朽
青春无可怀疑
白色的海洋穿过黎明的医院
轻盈的钢铁叙述着
锈蚀已久的夏天

2003

White Sea

A white sea courses through the hospital before dawn
Traces of warmth linger on naked glass
I lie on the wet sidewalk
its concrete surface icy as a mirror, the city
beneath my spine
running on silently

In the lowest depths of pain
it can only be night
My sleep bears the name of all deep sleep
My tears are all of the tears there are
The balm of lyricism
lifts the cover on lies

The universe is easily corrupted
but youth is beyond reproach
A white sea courses through the hospital before dawn
while supple steel gives an account
of a summer long fallen into rust

2003

花卉的时间

花卉的时间，玻璃的黑夜
冰冷的骨殖清晰可见
太阳割下的碎片正在返回
无瞳的双眼缓缓睁开

灵魂总有栖身之所
在茂盛的黑暗深处
像一株麦穗，逃亡者倚住
窄窄的梯子，悄无声息地生长

午夜的钟声如泣如诉
沙粒低低地跳跃着
今夜又是不绝的黑暗
城市在我的身边静寂无声

2002

Time of Flowers

Time of flowers, black night of glass
Icy skeletons sharply focused
Shards cut by the sun return
Eyes without pupils slowly open

The soul always has a place to shelter
in the lush depths of the darkness
Like an ear of wheat, a fugitive leans
on a narrow ladder, growing in silence

Midnight bells toll mournfully
Grains of sand rustle as they dance
Tonight is yet another round of endless darkness
The city beside me lies quiet and still

2002

终于有了昨日

终于有了昨日
终于有了愤怒
梦境终于有了核心
革命终于像一种日常生活
今天和今夜终于紧紧地葬在一起

已故的青春
已故的青春之论
暴风角多么像一只倾斜的杯子
傍晚的镜子不再把我描绘成幽灵
洗尽了的世界对我一无用处
缄默的石头，我的教师
温柔的才华
遵从着早已安排停当的命运
遵循这愤怒的预言
开始这无法结束的远征

我，我们，我们这多变的时代
星辰跟随着各自的神祇
转动着颈项

2001

At Last There Is Yesterday

At last there is yesterday
At last there is fury
Dreams now have a core
Revolution resembles something like normal life at last
Today and tonight are buried together entwined at last

Youth gone from this world
The very idea of youth gone from this world
The horn of the storm looks like a tilted cup
Evening's mirror no longer sketches me as a ghost
A world washed clean is useless to me
Silent stones, my teachers
those gentle talents
who comply with the fate arranged for them
bowing to this angry prophecy
setting out on a journey they will never complete

I, we, this mutable era of ours
Each star follows its own god
as it turns its head

2001

灰光灯

这声音里有阳光
这骨头里有歌声
这灯光里有透明的空隙
这红裙里有雨
这舞蹈里有血

不是八月，不必如此寡言
不是深秋，不必像海洋那样不住地叹息
暮色盛开的花朵
蝴蝶为露水所湿
如同天堂的眼睛

1998

Limelight / Greylight

There's sunlight in this voice
There's a song in these bones
There's a transparent gap in this lamplight
There's rain in this red dress
and blood in this dance

It isn't August, there's no need to stay silent
It isn't autumn, there's no need to sigh like the sea
Flowers that blossom in the dusk
Butterflies wet with dew
are like the eyes of heaven

1998

秋天的气味

雨水落到嘴唇上，仿佛消毒药水在漫延
刚刚浇铸过的柏油马路
水泥护栏变得苍白干燥
焚烧树叶和报纸的烟雾
沿着车厢内壁飘浮的面包芳香迎面而来
地狱和天堂的气味就是这样只是一线之隔
书页的气味，蠹虫的气味
猫贴近火炉，皮毛烤焦的气味
手指上的墨痕，在竹篮里腐烂的水果皮
香水在河堤下流淌
骤暗的天空挥发着酒精
明亮而坚韧的蛛网颤抖着横过河道
一根电话线通向我的城市
社区的心脏弥漫着煤气的臭味
雨水照亮的屋顶是惟一的来信
空巷映照着月光
秋天凋落的头发
悄悄落到抽屉的深处

2002

The Scent of Autumn

Rain falls on my lips, spreads like disinfectant
across a newly poured asphalt road
Cement railings turn pallid and dry
Smoke from burning leaves and newspapers
The scent of bread drifts along the interior wall of a train
    car to me
The smells of heaven and hell are just like this, divided by
    the thinnest line
The scent of books, the smell of bookworms
A cat presses close to a furnace, smell of scorched skin and
    fur
Ink stains on fingertips, rotten fruit peels in a bamboo
    basket
Perfume flows past the embankment
Suddenly darkened skies are vaporizing alcohol
Bright and resilient, a spider web bridging the river quakes
a phone line connecting my city
The neighborhood's heart saturated with the stench of coal
    gas
A rooftop shining with rain is the only letter that arrives
Empty lane lit up by moonlight
Autumn's withered hair
falls quietly into the recesses of a drawer

2002

没有爱情的日子

没有爱情的日子
我躺在无帆的桅杆下
我的身边坐满我的祖先
若有所思的灰色大海
缓缓注满透明的杯子

昏睡的我漂泊在海鸟的寂静中
无用的诗歌
紧握着松软的石头
冬天的伤口
为柔弱的玫瑰所缝补
疲倦的手指贴近临水的星辰
袖中的风暴犹如感伤的水银

遥远的幸福像一把尖刀
无休止地割着我的脚跟

1993.2.23

Days Without Love

Days without love
I lie beneath a mast without sails
my ancestors crowding around me
lost in thought, and the grey sea
slowly fills a transparent glass

Listlessly I drift among the stillness of seabirds
Useless poetry
clings to loose stones
Winter's wounds
sewn together by tender roses
Exhausted fingers almost touching the stars that skim the
    water
the storm fills my sleeves like grieving mercury

Distant happiness like a sharp knife
slicing at my heels

February 23, 1993

闲人街上的虱子

闲人街上的虱子
就像食饼的疯子,肉体格外轻盈
在倾斜的暴风雨中
踮着脚走过门外的回廊
像革命,像新闻
它告诉我命运的秘密
它的声音震撼我的耳膜

脸上贴着金箔
在瓷盘上反复交叉着前腿
悠闲地吞云吐雾
闲人街上的虱子
它的一生就是一种象征
它最后飘浮在咖啡杯中的时候
行将溺死的青年的脸
闪现诡谲的笑容
跟随着这盛满阳光的方舟驶向天堂

这启迪我的生物,我惟一的教师
从来是沉默的石头
但却有着至高无上的命运

1999

Louse on Idlers' Street

The louse on Idlers' Street
is like a madman eating cake, uncommonly nimble
in the driving rain
tripping down a winding arcade
Like the Revolution, like the news
it tells me the secret of destiny
its voice shaking my eardrums

Face covered in gold leaf
crossing its forelegs again and again on a porcelain basin
languidly blowing clouds of smoke
Louse on Idlers' Street
its entire life a symbol
When at last it floats into a cup of coffee
poised to drown, its youthful face
flashes a crafty smile
and follows that sunlit ark to Heaven

This enlightening creature, my only teacher
has always been a silent stone
that possesses nonetheless the loftiest of destinies

1999

明亮的仲夏夜

明亮的仲夏夜
蚁群包围着坠地的花朵
盐粒就像月色，树心
腐烂的巨株
透露出衰朽的气质

各种命运近在咫尺
冰冷的时间，可以看见骨头
无法舞蹈的手
不得不抚摸尘嚣颤栗的头发

明亮的仲夏夜
紧张的中心
我们面对的困难
同样包围着年代久远的前辈

眼睛凝视着寂静
免于明天的威胁

1997

Bright Midsummer Night

Bright midsummer night
Swarming ants besiege fallen blossoms
Grain of salt like the moon, a thick tree
with rotten heartwood
leaks an air of decay

Assorted destinies lie within our grasp
and in frigid times, you can see hands
with bones that can't dance
powerless to not caress the riot of shivering hair

Bright midsummer night
anxious center
The difficulties we face
besieged our forebears in the distant past

Eyes fixed on stillness
elude tomorrow's threats

1997

由于阴谋，由于顺从

由于阴谋，由于顺从
恐惧的今天，也就是
同样恐惧的明天

时间穿着唯一的旧靴子
候鸟向南飞去时，北方的冰山
倍感孤独

太阳教育并且凝固了我们的生活
小小的赞美诗左右着
苦难的星辰，泪水靠近的大海
悲剧已平淡无奇

2002

Because of Conspiracy, Because of Obedience

Because of conspiracy, because of obedience
today and its terror will be
the same terror tomorrow

Time wears the only old boots it has
When migrating birds fly south, the icebergs in the north
will feel even more alone

The sun instructs and hardens our lives
Little hymns control
the miserable stars, the oceans dogged by tears
Tragedy has become mundane

2002

最近七年

最近七年，严寒统一了边境
白色烧灼着我的生活
癫狂的盐粒，死在贵族的杯中

白天的火光，免疫的失落
活着的面包，活着的清水
送给我无法给予自己的部分

雾霭的背后，怀疑不可胜数
激情的尺度无所事事
雨水中的街巷变幻形体
混乱的城市充满苟活的毅力

2001

These Seven Years

These past seven years, a punishing cold has unified the
    borders
Whiteness scorches my life
a crazed grain of salt, dying in an aristocrat's cup

Daytime firelight, loss of immunity
Living bread, living fresh water
give me those portions I cannot give myself

Behind the fog, suspicions multiply
The eager yardstick has nothing to occupy itself
A rainy alley changes shape
This chaotic city overflows with striving come to
    wretchedness

2001

水手失去爱情

水手失去爱情，眼见航船慢慢沉没
国王坐在王座上，可是他的国家正在灭亡
在尘土飞扬的街道上
我掏出手帕仔细端详白色的纤维

泪水这辆马车没有驭手
也没有车轮
但有疾风吹送着它无边的痛苦
进入春天的阴影

1995

The Mariner Loses His Love

The mariner loses his love, watches his ship slowly sink
The king sits on his throne, as his country is laid waste
On the road with its swirling dust
I take out a handkerchief, examine the white fibers

Tears are a chariot without a driver
and without wheels
but there's a strong wind blowing its endless suffering
into the shadows of spring

1995

惧色

黎明的结构
露水般清澈
光芒如同秀美的脚踝
向明亮集中
平安的缄默
自己的灯
避难的项链
预言的信徒
复活的小麦
父亲树上的叶子
甜蜜的黄金
风暴流露着
悲痛的激情
世界的末日，百无禁忌
忙碌的奇迹
在梦的终结处

2001

Fear

The structure of dawn
transparent as dew
Rays of light like graceful ankles
gather into the brilliance
The reticence of peace
one's own lamp
a necklace seeking asylum
Believers in the prophecy
wheat reborn
The leaves on father tree
honey-sweet gold
The storm exposes
the intensity of grief
On the last day of the world, nothing is forbidden
A flurry of miracles
at the terminus of a dream

2001

我又一次说到风暴

我又一次说到风暴
是因为我酷爱这个词
酷爱这词语中燃烧的热度
酷爱在唇齿之间跳跃的火星

90度的阴凉，潮湿灌木下的宝藏
无忧无虑的饕餮之徒
夸夸其谈的年轻人
还有放荡的叛徒全都翩然而至

上帝的手指已经疲惫不堪
让我们一起去灯光明亮的地方吧
在随后的命运中，谁知道还将轮到
哪一种声音来主宰众生的智慧

我又一次说到风暴
是因为我要像它一样继续自命不凡
我愿意和它一起蔑视道德的力量
目睹帝国崩溃前最后的一瞬

2004

I Speak of the Storm Again

I speak of the storm again
because I love this word intensely
love the heat that burns inside it
love the sparks that dance on lips and teeth

Ninety degrees in the shade, precious ore hidden under
    damp thickets
Carefree gluttons
bombastic youths
and sleazy traitors float on over

God has worked his fingers to the bone
getting us to go where the lights are bright
In the fate that remains, who knows what kind of
voice will preside over the wisdom of all living things

I speak of the storm again
because I want to be like it and regard myself as above the
    fray
I want to share its contempt for the power of morality
and witness with my own eyes the final instant before the
    empire crashes down

2004

A Summer Day in the
Company of Ghosts

(1990–1993)

说多了就是威胁

说多了就是威胁，朋友
但是，不要忘记笑
不要忘记毛病总在车轮中
不要忽略难以避免的同行的忧伤
不要让破损的友谊
像桌上的水迹那样消隐

说吧，保持无可替代的嫉妒
用这只手去征服
另一只同样激烈的手

抛向空中的分币必须有正反两面
亲爱的朋友，说多了就是威胁
说对了，就是死亡

1991.6.24

To Say More Would Be Risky

To say more would be risky, my friend
But don't forget to laugh
Don't forget the flaw is in the wheel
Don't neglect the inevitable grief of colleagues
Don't let damaged friendships
fade away like traces of water on a tabletop

Speak, hold onto your irreplaceable hatred
Use this hand to conquer
the other equally fierce one

A coin tossed into the air must have two sides
Dear friend, to say more would be risky
To speak the truth, that would be death

June 24, 1991

送斧子的人来了

送斧子的人来了
斧子来了

低飞的绳索
缓缓下降的砖瓦木屑
在光荣中颤栗

送斧子的人来了
斧子的微笑
一如四季的轮转
岁月的肌肤
抹得油亮

被绳索锁住的呜咽
穿过恐惧
终于切开夜晚的镜面

送斧子的人来了
斧子的歌曲中断在它的使命中

送斧子的人来了
我们的头来了

1991.9.4

The Man with the Axe Is Here

The man with the axe is here
The axe is here

Low-flying rope
slowly raining bricks and tiles and sawdust
shudder in the glory

The man with the axe is here
The axe's smile
like the revolving seasons
The skin of years
rubbed to an oily sheen

Fettered by ropes, liquid keening
bores through dread
slicing open the mirror of night

The man with the axe is here
the axe's song cut off mid-mission

The man with the axe is here
Our heads are here

September 4, 1991

鹈鹕

顺着昨天和今天的潮水
我们正在靠近那只鹈鹕
向前倾斜的身影
比划艇的尖端更早地触及
沉浸在水里的黄色尖喙
和鸟翅下深藏的黑暗

我们尽可能近地靠近那只
鹈鹕，它却已腾空而起
水面上响起利器跌倒的声音

木桨在膝上滴下的水珠
割开阳光粗大的颗粒
在它离去之后
在失去寂静的寂静之中
仿佛解冻的灵魂
我们缓缓苏醒

1990

Pelican

Following the tides of yesterday and today
we approach the pelican
our shadows tipped before us
ahead of the rowboat's sharp prow to touch
the sharp yellow beak underwater
and the darkness harbored in the depths of its wings

Just as we draw close
the pelican takes wing and rises into the air
the sound of a blade falling on the water

Beads of water drip from oars to knees
splitting open coarse grains of sunlight
After it has gone
in the stillness that has lost its stillness
like frozen souls beginning to thaw
we slowly reawaken

1990

阳光

当阳光，当航船，当夏天炽热的兵器
倚靠着我们的脸，当我们
拥有难以隐蔽的喜悦
当我们的手不再疼痛
当我们衰弱躯体中的思想终于完美

我们也就会听见
在园艺师和金匠等待我们的房间里
蓝舌鸟嘀铭
犹如幽灵为生者默诵祷文
喷泉之后的树林之中
另一些携蛇仗的人已经到来
这一切就像水，来而复去
充满智慧却永不结果

当航船驶去，当阳光黯淡
当夏天的号角又一次吹起
这对季节的欢呼，也就是
我们自身最好的赞颂

1990

Sunlight

When sunlight, when boats, when summer's scorching weapons
    weapons
lean into our faces, when we
harbor joy that's hard to conceal
when our hands stop aching
when the thoughts inside our weak bodies achieve
    perfection at last

then we will be able to hear
in a room where gardener and goldsmith await us
blue-tongued birds singing
like ghosts chanting prayers for the living
In the woods behind the fountain
other people have already arrived, bearing caducei
All of this is like water, coming in, then going away
bursting with wisdom but never bearing fruit

When boats cast off, when sunlight dims
when summer's horn sounds again
heralding the season, this is
for us, the best benediction

1990

风暴

风暴将临的呼吸隐约可闻
飞蝇压弯草茎
门窗不再来回拍打
咖啡颤抖着
托盘上冰凉的瓷杯更加洁白

已无所谓什么征兆
风暴就是一切
凡是上帝的赐予
我都毫不畏惧
而他对我殷勤的回报
却永无回答

风暴折断的翅膀
遍布胆汁的颜色
生死依然模糊不清
唯有无言的祈祷
发自内心

1991.10.2

Storm

The storm is about to break, we hear its faint breathing
Grasses bend under swarming flies
Doors and windows stop banging back and forth
Coffee shivers
Cold porcelain cups turn whiter on the tray

We've stopped caring about omens
The storm is everything
Whatever God might give me
doesn't frighten me at all
The retribution he's contrived for me
will forever go unanswered

Wings broken by the storm
are the color of bile
Life and death blur together
Only wordless prayers
escape from my heart

October 2, 1991

和幽灵在一起的夏日

和幽灵在一起的夏日
阳光沐浴着悲伤的色彩
预言的自行车
陪伴着先人种植已久的城镇

英雄极度过剩
度量破坏殆尽
日常事件痛苦不堪
礼仪麻木不仁

主要的河流和次要的海水
近乎梦幻般的交融
太多的神祇
已使季节几成谎言

疯狂的睡莲在黎明开放
木桨柔软如同蝶翅
和夏日在一起的幽灵
狂跳的心充满忧虑

1991.1

A Summer Day in the Company of Ghosts

A summer day in the company of ghosts
While sunlight bathes mournful colors
prophetic bicycles
join ancestors sown in long-ago towns

Too many heroes to count
They've crushed every scale
everyday events too painful to bear
callous rituals leave us numb

Major rivers and minor seas
mingle like dreams
Too many gods
have rendered the season a lie

A frenzy of waterlilies blooms at dawn
Wooden oars soft as butterfly wings
A summer day in the company of ghosts
My wildly beating heart fills with anguish

January 1991

陡峭的时辰

受惑的个性依旧纯洁
思想终于淹没了行动
头发中红色的蛇信
指向风暴的终点
横跨栅栏的光芒
发自寓言的远端

每一段蔑视的时代
每一根命运的神经
每一朵太阳下的向日葵
每一种今天的牺牲品
是最神秘的意会
是赞歌的沉默

1991.11.22

Precipitous Hours

The gullible remain pure
Thoughts drown action in the end
Red snake tongues in my hair
point towards the terminus of the storm
Rays of light spanning the fences
have traveled from the distant side of a fable

Every scornful era
every fateful nerve
every sunflower under the sun
every one of today's sacrificial objects
are the most mysterious of epiphanies
are the muteness of praise songs

November 22, 1991

神赐

你将如何感谢落日，天才
你将如何看待这些政治的玫瑰
这些毫无主见的春天

你将如何倾听时针的暴动
如何应付纸中的火
城市之下汹涌的河流

袖中的幻景
越过了合理的界限
病人的目光和旗帜的狂笑
这样相似
承诺如此虚假
隐秘如此迅捷

忧伤的头骨，夏日的心
悲痛的芬芳，还有
天河那边孩子们的哭声

你又将如何才能回答

1992

Gifts from On High

How will you thank the setting sun, God-given talents
How will you come to see these roses of politics
these springtimes bereft of independent thought

How will you listen for the hour hand's insurrection
What will you do about the flames burning through paper
or the raging river that surges beneath the city

The illusions hidden up your sleeves
exceed the limits of reason
The sick man's gaze and the cackling of banners
are so very alike
Promises are so hollow
and secrets so nimble

Grieving skulls, the heart of a summer day
sorrowful fragrances, along with
the cries of children in the Milky Way

How can you ever answer

1992

我的前生是一个补鞋匠

我的前生是一个补鞋匠
他的户籍在城市登记簿某一页的最后一行
我所有的情欲和幻想
全部来自他长年衔住铁钉而变得黝黑的嘴唇
这嘴唇犹如泥土之下麦子黑暗的根部
他探出地窖的双眼
天天盯住来来往往的皮鞋和马靴
想象着裙裾之中温暖的小腿
我的前生，像个业余哲学家
在贴近地面的地方更多地听到宇宙的声音
听到空洞如何吞噬潮汐
听到飓风如何毁灭村庄

我的前生是一个补鞋匠
我常常在百货公司的玻璃窗上看到他的笑容
他越过如此多拥挤的灵魂向着我微笑
他留给我的不是银面具
而是乌黑的头发和发动机般有力的双手
他是我珍藏中的一双干手爪
是未兑现的彩票号码
是向着星辰的一声凄厉狞笑
革命曾使他惊醒
但又很快被不朽的皇帝砍去头颅

In a Past Life I Was a Cobbler

In a past life I was a cobbler
His household was entered on the last line of a page in the
    city register
All of my desires and dreams
issued from his lips, blackened from years of clamping
    down on iron nails
lips like the dark roots of wheat beneath the earth
His eyes peered out from a cellar
fixed on the daily parade of leather shoes and riding boots
He imagined the warm calves beneath all those skirts
In a past life, like an amateur philosopher
close to the ground, hearing the sounds of the universe
listening to the way empty spaces swallow up the tides
listening to the way hurricanes lay waste to villages

In a past life I was a cobbler
I often see his smiling face in department store windows
moving towards me through a press of spirits, smiling
He left me not a silver mask
but raven hair and hands as strong as engines
He's a pair of ragged claws for my collection
a lottery ticket that's still unredeemed
a gale of shrill laughter aimed at the stars
The Revolution stirred him
but he was soon put to death by the immortal Emperor
His sopping wet head on a platter
he had to let curs lick the rain from his face

他在盘子里湿淋淋的脑袋
只能任由野狗舔尽脸上的雨水

我的前生是一个补鞋匠
我最大的压抑是不让他知道
我对他怀有无限的自豪和仇恨
我的臭不可闻的前生
肩扛手提从活人脚上剥下的一串串鞋子
将他的秘密断断续续地传授给我
他每一次伪造他远离尘世的死亡
他的嘴里就会掉下一枚铁钉
我只得锁在屋子里从窗帘后面
看他被愤怒的醉汉和主妇追逐

我的前生是一个补鞋匠
他的裁缝朋友今天依然是裁缝
慈眉善目的花匠依然是花匠
但他们在各自的大理石浴缸里
像威严的贵族那样腰背笔直
手臂平举，远远地端详早晨的报纸
只有我成了诗人，在一个早晨
尾随夏日的火星，乘坐一辆无轨电车驶向闹市中心
我的身边，城市中勤劳的人们
从倾斜的缺口进入这片明亮干净的低地

1993

In a past life I was a cobbler
The greatest pressure I feel is to keep him from knowing
the pride and hatred I harbor towards him
In my stinking past life
I carried strings of shoes peeled from the feet of the living
which have meted out his secrets to me
Each time he faked his death and pretended to leave this
    world of dust
another iron nail would fall from his mouth
I can only stay locked indoors and sit by the window
Watching an angry drunk and a housewife chase him down

In a past life I was a cobbler
His tailor friend is still a tailor
the kind-faced gardener is still a gardener
but each of them sits in his own marble bathtub
straight-backed and dignified like an aristocrat
perusing the morning paper at arms' length
Trailing the Red Planet on a summer day, riding a trolley
    that speeds towards downtown
Beside me, people who toil in the heart of the city
pass through a diagonal slash to enter its bright, clean
    lowlands

1993

你的命运

在平静的前夕　在黎明的中心
在伟大的尘埃中
在你如星光般纤弱的手心

风暴的背面就是你的命运
烛光落在眼睑里
剪刀打开草药的心
亡魂列车在你身边缓缓而行
莫测的马蹄
反复踏着昏迷已久的水面

你的命运
在风暴的背面
在灵魂的日子里
在利斧的寂静中

1991.6.27

Your Fate

In the quiet of the night before   in the heart of dawn
in the immensity of the dust
in the palm of your hand, delicate as starlight

Beyond the storm, there lies your fate
Candlelight falls on your eyelids
Scissors break open the heart of a remedy
A ghost train rolls slowly beside you
Enigmatic horse hooves
crisscross the dazed surface of the waters

Your fate
is beyond the storm
In the days of the soul
in the silence of an axe

June 27, 1991

Recitation

(1981–1987)

想起一部捷克电影但想不起片名

鹅卵石街道湿漉漉的
布拉格湿漉漉的
公园拐角上姑娘吻了你
你的眼睛一眨不眨
后来面对枪口也是这样
党卫军雨衣反穿
像光亮的皮大衣
三轮摩托驶过
你和朋友们倒下的时候
雨还在下
我看见一滴雨水和另一滴雨水
在电线上追逐
最后掉到鹅卵石路上
我想起你
嘴唇动了动
没有人看见

1983

Thinking about a Czech Film, but
I Can't Remember the Title

Cobblestone streets, soaking wet
Prague, soaking wet
On a corner by the park a girl kisses you
You do not blink
Later as you face the guns you still don't blink
Waffen-SS rain slickers inside out
like shiny leather overcoats
A three-wheeled motorbike speeds by
When you and your friends fall to the ground
rain is still falling
I see one raindrop and another raindrop
chasing along a powerline
and finally tumbling to the cobblestone road
I think of you
lips moving
No one sees

1983

英国人

英国人幽默有余

大腹便便有余

做岛民有余

英国人那时候造军舰有余

留长鬓角扛毛瑟枪有余

打印度人打中国人有余

英国人草场有余

海洋有余

罗宾汉有余鲁滨逊有余

英国人现在泰晤士河里沉船有余

海德公园铁栏有余

催泪弹罢工有余

英国人塞巴斯蒂安·科的长腿有余

列侬的长发有余

戴安娜王妃的婚礼长裙有余

英国人也就是行车靠左有余

也就是伦敦浓雾有余

也就是英国人有余有余有余

1983

The English

The English have humor in abundance
pot bellies in abundance
island-dwellers in abundance
The English once built warships in abundance
wore long sideburns and carried Mausers in abundance
beat down Indians and beat down Chinese in abundance
The English have lawns in abundance
oceans in abundance
Robin Hoods in abundance Robinson Crusoes in abundance
The English now have sunken ships in the River Thames
    in abundance
Hyde Park's wrought iron in abundance
tear gas and strikes in abundance
The English have Sebastian Coe's long legs in abundance
Lennon's long hair in abundance
Princess Diana's wedding gown in abundance
The English do indeed drive on the left side of the road in
    abundance
indeed the heavy fogs of London are abundant
indeed the English are abundant are abundant are abundant

1983

红色旅馆

我死后，我死了

以后，你看他们就在我的书架上
随随便便地翻着
看看我的藏书

你看他们就在弹烟灰的时候
吐出一两句笑话
扯扯竖起的风衣领子

你看我待在一个黑色的小匣子
一本黑色的诗集
一颗黑色的行星里
陌生而且寒冷

你看他们这样自然地用
手枪敲打这黑的颜色

最初的几秒钟是寂静的
你看房门被风打开
你看他们所有的白色眼睛贴着绿墙倒塌
你看他们的血沾在靴子上
然后再被踏在地板上

1983

Red Hotel

After I die, I'll be dead

and then, you'll see them by my bookshelves
leafing casually through the pages
perusing my library

You'll see them flicking ash from their cigarettes
cracking a joke or two
windbreaker collars turned up

You'll see me inside a little black case
a black-bound book of poems
in a black planet
foreign and cold

You'll see how naturally they use
pistols to strike this black color

The first few seconds are calm
You'll see the doors thrown open by the wind
You'll see all of their white staring eyes glued to the
    collapsing green walls
You'll see their blood soaking their boots
once again tracked across the floor

1983

罗伯特·卡巴

一个战地摄影记者对我说
雨停了
真的，我们从拐角的餐厅出来
雨停了
只是有了风

但是湄公河三角洲却一直在下雨
三周以后他就死在那儿
死在黑色的雨季
他的脸上从没有伤痕
没有
最后倒在芭蕉树下的时候
也没有
他的左手像握着自己的右手优美地
握着照相机
一片暗绿色的树叶柔软地
在黑皮靴黑夹克上闪耀

当我和他从餐厅出来
雨后的天上
有一块深褐色的斑点
像卡巴夹克衫上的纽扣
不过我们谁也没有说

1983

Robert Capa

A war photographer said to me
The rain stopped
It's true, when we stepped out of the corner café
the rain had stopped
and the wind picked up

But it kept on raining in the Mekong River Delta
Three weeks later he died there
died in the black rainy season
his face unscarred
unmarked
and in the end when he fell at the base of a plantain
he was still unmarked
As if gracefully clasping his right, his left hand
held his camera
A wall of dark green leaves shimmered
softly on his black leather boots and black jacket

When he and I left the café
the sky after the rain
had one brown spot
like a buttonhole in Capa's jacket
But neither of us spoke of it

1983

我们如此成功

我们如此成功

跨越阳台栏杆跨越鸟巢

只是撩一下衣服下摆

我们如此成功

从高高的跳台上落下

跳伞的尼龙里层一片黑暗

我们如此成功

北半球的太阳

刚刚照亮大大小小的冰山

我们如此成功

如此成功地登上这月球般荒凉的表面

诗人加里·施奈德

坐在那条山路的尽头

天色微明看不清

他是不是还留着络腮胡子

他脱下鞋子倒出一些沙子

马上有一阵风

也吹起他的头发

乌鸦的头发

月球上的风也敲打鼓点

有风并没有什么

只是突然感到

人生来就是一种动物

1984

We've Accomplished So Much

We've accomplished so much
vaulting over balcony railings vaulting over birds' nests
We just hike up our clothes
We've accomplished this much
leaping from high platforms
completely dark inside the nylon parachute lining
We're so accomplished
and the northern sun
just lit up a field of icebergs large and small
We've achieved so much
successfully climbing a height as desolate as the surface of
   the moon
Gary Snyder
resting on a mountain at the end of a trail
the brightening sky too dim
to reveal whether or not he still wears a full beard
He takes off his shoes and pours out some sand
and just then a gust of wind
ruffles his hair
raven black hair
The lunar wind also taps a drumbeat
The wind itself devoid of any meaning
but the sudden sensation
that human beings are just another kind of animal

1984

与诗人勃莱一夕谈

夜色中的草很深
很久没有人迹
很久没有想起你了
你的孤立的下巴闪烁
像天上那颗红色的星

除了夜晚还得在深草中静坐
交叠手指
以便忘记黎明来临
忘记已告别书本多年

一匹白马迎面而来，一只白蝴蝶
踏过虫声萤光

1984

Talking Through the Night with Robert Bly

Thick grasses in the night
No one has left footprints here in a long time
I haven't thought about you in a long time
your solitary chin flickering
like that red star up in the sky

All night you must sit in the tall grass and meditate
fingers laced
to forget the approaching dawn
to forget that you bid farewell to books so many years ago

A white horse approaches you, a white butterfly
treading the radiance of insect song

1984

阳光

阳光在我宽阔的衣领上移动
他们也是有生命的
我们都在户外，相距很近
他们也是有生命的
他们知道我在想些什么
下一个动作是什么
他们生存或不生存在树叶上
都和人相似
都是大段的、苍白的独白
他们也是有生命的
而最终他们又消失了
我们还活着
活着，重归黑暗

1985

Sunlight

Rays of sunlight move over my wide collar
They too have lives
We're all outside, not far apart
They too have lives
They know what I am thinking
what my next move will be
Their existence or absence on the leaves
is very human
All those drawn out and haggard monologues
they too have lives
but in the end, they will disappear again
and we'll still be alive
alive, to return to the darkness

1985

读书

室外好像每天都在下雨
读书，埋头于书本犹如推土机
我推着半截子书前进
再也不可能被谁任意战胜
书已成为书了，我还活着
眼瞧着他们年深日久了
表情忧郁，颜色发灰
像深色马的鬃毛梳理得整整齐齐
室外好像每天都在下雨
他们也沉思默想
他们又埋头干什么

1985

Studying

Outside, it seems like it's always raining
Studying, head buried in books like a bulldozer
I push half a load of books forward
No one's going to pick a fight with me again
The books have been bound into books, and I'm still alive
You can tell just by looking that they're getting on in years
Their expressions are brooding, their color ashen
well-combed like the groomed manes of chestnut horses
Outside it seems like it's always raining
They are deep in thought
Why are they burying their heads yet again?

1985

致梁晓明

如同又在列车的车厢中不期而遇

如同一片阳光移向另一片阳光

如同我们各自的马聆听月色消溶

如同窗外升起一株盛开的梨树

如同切开了的松果和完整的松果香气弥漫

如同我无法松开我的头发你已开始旋舞

如同房屋的后背总是空的

如同所有的镜子都有裂缝

如同我变成一个影子你也变成一个影子

在同一张纸上
你的手放在我的手边

1986

To Liang Xiaoming

Just as one meets by chance on a train

Just as a patch of sunlight moves towards another patch of
      sunlight

Just as each of our horses listens carefully to the melting
      moonlight

Just as a pear tree in full bloom rises outside the window

Just as cut open pinecones and whole pinecones spread
      their scent

Just as I can't untie my hair while you're already spinning
      around

Just as the back of the room is always empty

Just as every mirror is cracked

Just as I become a shadow you too become shadow

On the same sheet of paper
your hand rests beside mine

1986

马

我的马在雨中独自回家
它的毛色像我满布伤痕的右手
我的马双目微闭
迈着细步回家

我喝着酒，隔着酒馆的长窗
只能看到它瘦削的侧面
它正在回家，像我沉默时一样低着头
但远比我像个绅士

而我要远行，两眼通红
坐在酒液乱流的桌旁
看着我的马
在雨中独自回家

1987.6.7

Horse

My horse heads home alone in the rain
its coat the color of my scarred right hand
The eyes of my horse are half closed
as it walks with small steps, heading home

Drinking wine, beside the picture window of the wine shop
I see only its thin and bony silhouette
It's heading home, head lowered like mine when I'm silent
but so much more a gentleman than me

And I will travel far away, my eyes bloodshot
Sitting at this table with its splashes of spilled wine
watching my horse
head home alone in the rain

June 7, 1987

信

你的信像一只张着的耳朵
我提着它走过市场
你一定听见了许多此地方言
很多江南的细微尘埃

我不时踩到它的影子
我的这部分告诉你是我提着你

空气中裂开一条缝
它的句子已开始出错
沟渠河道里游鱼闪闪发光

它夹在我的书本里
不停地转动着耳轮

我要打电话给你
让你早早取回

1987

Letter

Your letter is like an open ear
I carry it through the marketplace
You can hear our local language
the fine silt of Jiangnan

I keep stepping on its shadow
This part tells you that I'm carrying you

Torn by the air
its sentences become filled with errors
Fish swimming in the canal shimmer and glint

It's pressed inside one of my books
endlessly circling the ear's auricle

I want to call you on the phone
so you'll hurry home

1987

大陆新村9号

上海的冬天
难得有雪
他写过的五个夜晚
又悄然回来
像五个女人
温柔地飘落在他的肩头
他闭上双眼，合上手
一棵树又一棵树
静静地静静地
落满了雪
安然熟睡

长夜漫漫长夜漫漫
漫漫

1985

[注：上海山阴路大陆新村9号为鲁迅故居。]

No. 9 New Continental Village

Shanghai winters
rarely see snow
Those five nights he wrote about
have silently returned
like five women
drifting softly around his shoulders
He closes his eyes, clasps his hands
One tree and then another
quietly, quietly
shrouded in snow
sleeping peacefully

Long nights neverending night neverending
neverending

1985

Author's note: No. 9 New Continental Village, on Shanyin Road
in Shanghai, is a former residence of the writer Lu Xun (1881–
1936).

5号

书架打开了书本打开了
纸张迎风飘动
劈劈啪啪，火星四溅
盛夏黄昏的许多小虫子
许多焦糊味
风吹动树叶吹动
蝴蝶的翅膀吹动
面容成为一条土星的光环
在此之间孤独的星球孤独的我
痛苦万分

1983

#5

Bookcase opened books opened
pages flutter in the wind
cascade of crackling sparks
So many insects in the high summer dusk
so heavy the smell of charring
Wind stirs the leaves of the trees stirs
butterfly wings tickles
a face and becomes a halo around the Earth
In the midst of this a lonely planet my lonely self
in great pain

1983

32号

玻璃长窗
隔开树荫下的
细致

表情和车铃

无沿软帽还有
自行车

滑过来又滑
过去或
者停住

室内的某一把调羹
重新放回到
桌布上

一片叶子沾满了阳光

1985

#32

Tall windows
blocked from the details
beneath shade trees

Facial expressions and bicycle bells

Soft caps along with
bicycles

gliding here and gliding
away or may-
be coming to a stop

Indoors a random spoon
newly returned to
the tabletop

A leaf saturated with sunlight

1985

House of Spirits

(1987–1988)

闯入者

闯入者　　总是在一侧
就像隔壁的地毯从门下伸入
爬向四壁
就像一扇门向里打开

缓缓抖动的扇子
夏日的火焰
别人的头发
纸上的字迹
盒中的针
餐桌前的第五把椅子
一只断手
无法找到其余部分的皮肉
闯入者那看不见的脸
一如钟表深奥的内部

在安静的同时
总有一种更安静的声音
正在靠近

我总是有所期待地盯着
杯子洁净的内壁

琴弦随时都张着

1987–88

Intruder

The intruder   always off to the side
like the neighbor's carpet peeking out under the door
creeping up the walls
like a door opening inward

A fan slowly shuddering
The flames of a summer day
Hair from someone else's head
Traces of words on paper
Needles in a box
The fifth chair at a dining table
A severed hand
has no way to find the rest of its flesh
The intruder's invisible face
is like the dim interior of a wristwatch

Wherever there is tranquility
there is always an even more tranquil sound
drawing close

I'm always staring expectantly
at the spotless interior wall of glass

The strings of an instrument may grow taut at any moment

1987–88

睡眠者

玻璃一样的脸
如一只水母
一片小城之光

黎明的黑暗深处
道路苍茫
和所有相遇的手交错而过
嘴唇张开融化在空气里面
肩膀在被单下了无痕迹
木盆盛满皂液
鞋子陷入沙中
偶然的梦
像野外的床
像一朵花转向无意的方向
你梦见我
梦见我脸上
也长出玻璃
这一切都因为有了风的缘故

黎明时分
道路苍茫
卡车偶尔驶过
你也像树叶上撒落的雨
颤抖不止

1987–88

Sleeper

Face like glass
like a jellyfish
the glow of a small town

In the depths of predawn darkness
streets wide and deserted
Brushing past each hand
lips open and melt into the air
No trace at all of shoulders beneath the bedding
wooden basin filled with liquid soap
shoes sink into the sand
a random dream
like an outdoor bed
like a flower turning towards indifference
you dream of me
dream that my face
has grown a layer of glass
all because the wind has come up

Before dawn
the streets are desolate
A solitary truck drives past
and just like the rain spattering the leaves
you can't stop trembling

1987–88

梦游者

读着古希腊的诗下楼
像一枚戒指
读着诗缓缓而下
充满馨香

行走已使她受伤，她的
右脚哭泣不止
她的眼睛似不落的白昼
照耀着磨损已久的庭院
和院中的水罐

两个迷路人，另一个是谁
陷在椅子里
没有一丝声息
她心中隐隐的痛苦
她的手指印痕
在门廊暗处
深藏不露

列队出巢的蜜蜂
抬起透明的古老泥土
裹着她的影子

1987–88

Sleepwalker

Reading ancient Greek poetry, descending the stairs
worn like a ring
Reading poetry, descending so slowly
redolent of incense

Walking hurts her, her
right foot constantly weeping
Her eyes like unstopped daylight
illuminate the rundown garden
and courtyard cistern

Two lost souls, and who is the other one
sunk in a chair
not making a sound
She suffers in secret
her fingerprints
left in the dim recesses of the portico
hidden so deeply they never show

Bees leave the hive in formation
bearing translucent ancient mud
bundling up her shadow

1987–88

火星人

他们给我橙色的冰块
一艘同样颜色的飞船
他们和我共饮桌上的茶
共享盒中的饼干
他们捏起我的书籍
像提起空气的一角
教我踏过水上的火焰

只有他们，我这唯一的三个朋友
树叶般轻扬的朋友
如同音乐涂上瓷器
又随着夜晚
在圆镜之外悄然褪去

1987–88

Martians

They gave me orange ice cubes
an airship the same color
They drank tea at the table with me
shared cookies from a tin
They pincered my books
as if lifting a corner of air
and taught me to walk across embers on the water

No one but them, my only three friends
my friends as light as leaves
like music-painted porcelain
and once again with the night
they quietly withdrew beyond the mirror moon

1987–88

纸人

我有的是纸
可以做想要的一切

做出我的妻子
做出妻子尚未收集齐全的酒杯

做出她的外套
涂上她喜欢的红色
做出成套的家具
一幢住房，插满鲜艳的旗帜
易于搬迁

做出我们的富足和雨点
使它们转瞬即逝

做出我们的表情
便于撕毁

在我晚境将临之时
我把剩下的白纸
七张干净洁白的纸
摊在桌上
看着它们被太阳晒着
慢慢地融化

1987–88

Paper Man

What I have is paper
to make anything I want

Make my wife
Make the set of wineglasses she has yet to complete

Make her overcoat
tinted her favorite red
Make a suite of furniture
a place to live, festooned with bright banners
easy to relocate

Make our prosperity and raindrops
Make them vanish in the blink of an eye

Fashion our expressions
easily ripped to shreds

When I face the evening of life
I will take the paper that remains
seven clean white sheets
spread them on the table
watch them soak up the sunlight
and slowly melt away

1987–88

情 人

我们到海上了，亲爱的
岸上的灯火已经熄灭
海马的笛声婉转悠扬
我们到海上了
我打开你的盒子
把你撒下去
小块的你
比粉末更慢更慢地
在水面上斜斜地落下去
我把你全都撒下去了
你使海水微微发红
你使海洋平静了
如同你活着时
午夜的雪降落在
展开的手上
我把天空给你了
把海洋也给你了
都给你了　都给你了
我把装你的盒子
藏入怀中
我把我装入你的盒中
我在你的梦里了

1987–88

Lover

We have reached the open sea, my love
the shore lights extinguished
seahorse flutes sweet and lilting
We have reached the open sea
I open the urn
scatter you
little pieces of you
falling more slowly than powder
obliquely onto the water
I scatter all of you
You turn the sea faintly red
You calm the waters
just as when you were alive and
midnight snows fell upon
our open hands
I give you the sky
give you the sea
I give it all to you   all to you
I take the urn that held you
hold it to my breast
I put myself inside the urn that held you
I am now in your dreams

1987–88

TRANSLATOR'S ACKNOWLEDGMENTS

THIS BOOK would not have been possible without the support and friendship of many people. Many thanks to Wang Yin, whose trust in my understanding of his poems and in my ability to convey their objective and subjective sense in English has given me the freedom to do my best work. A shout out to Robin Visser, who first introduced me to the publisher and bookseller Yan Bofei, who in turn introduced me to Wang Yin. Thanks to Bofei and to Wu Yanting, who makes the best duck-and-winter-melon soup ever. I am deeply grateful to the numerous friends in Shanghai who have been generous with their hospitality over the years and opened many doors—my dear friends and Shanghai publishers Monika Lin and David Perry, Colleen Berry (who taught me how to text in Chinese on a flip phone), Mina Choi, Justin Denney, Diana Gu, Kristine Konopka, Monika Lin, Mian Mian, Sawako Nakayasu, and Ann Niu. I am also grateful to the collective minds of the Bay Area Literary Translators and Writers Group (you know who you are!), whose insightful readings and suggestions helped me shape the final versions of some of the poems in this collection. Special thanks to Wei Yang Menkus, who has always been generous with her time when I've been stumped by some fine point of usage or syntax, and to Daniel Tay, whose medical expertise was instrumental in finding a solution for a particular translation challenge. Many thanks to Jeffrey Yang, my editor at New York Review Books, whose enthusiasm for this project kept it on track through the pandemic, and whose sensitive readings and insightful suggestions helped me do my best work. Deepest appreciation to the rest of the production team at NYRB who have kept the presses rolling throughout. I would also like to express my gratitude to the Henry Luce Foundation, which supported the two-week translation residency Wang Yin and I spent at the Vermont Studio Center, which provided the space and time for me to complete the bulk of this manuscript, and to the warm and tireless staff at the center, including the intrepid Kathy Black. I dedicate this book to my children, who became adults during the years I was putting together these translations, and to my husband, Neil Henry—you bring light and warmth to every day.

SZILÁRD BORBÉLY In a Bucolic Land
Translated by Ottilie Mulzet

NAJWAN DARWISH Exhausted on the Cross
Translated by Kareem James Abu-Zeid; Foreword by Raúl Zurita

GLORIA GERVITZ Migrations: Poem, 1976–2020
Translated by Mark Schafer

SAKUTARŌ HAGIWARA Cat Town
Translated by Hiroaki Sato

MICHAEL HELLER Telescope: Selected Poems

LI SHANGYIN *Edited and translated by Chloe Garcia Roberts*

CLAIRE MALROUX Daybreak: New and Selected Poems
Translated by Marilyn Hacker

ARVIND KRISHNA MEHROTRA *Selected by Vidyan Ravinthiran;
Introduction by Amit Chaudhuri*

MELISSA MONROE Medusa Beach and Other Poems

VIVEK NARAYANAN After

ELISE PARTRIDGE The If Borderlands: Collected Poems

ALICE PAALEN RAHON Shapeshifter
Translated and with an introduction by Mary Ann Caws

ARTHUR RIMBAUD The Drunken Boat: Selected Writings
*Edited, translated, and with an introduction and notes by Mark
Polizzotti*

JACK SPICER After Lorca
Preface by Peter Gizzi

NACHOEM WIJNBERG *Translated by David Colmer*